Socialism Made Easy
James Connolly

Contents

FOREWORD

In this work the author presents his own views in his own manner. Hence he employs the first person singular in preference to the impersonal 'we' of journalism or of official production. The articles have been written at various times in Ireland and America and have already attained a wide circulation through being reprinted in various Socialist journals in both countries. Constant requests to the author to have them collected and published in a more permanent and accessible form have induced him to make this selection in the hope that they may be thought not unworthy of a place in at least the fugitive literature of the Socialist movement.

A word as to the plan of the work may not be amiss here. Section 1 is light, satirical, jesting and serious by turns, and follows the usual course of attack and defense, argument and rebuttal, experienced by a Socialist workman in factory, workshop or mine before he has destroyed the prejudices and won the serious consideration of his fellow workers. Section 2 is serious throughout, and is an attempt to deduce from actual every-day experiences and from historical facts the probable correct answer to the question put by the worker when he realizes the necessity of a change, viz: How must we act? How are we going to do it?

SECTION I - WORKSHOP TALKS

[INTERNATIONALISM]

SOCIALISM IS A FOREIGN IMPORTATION!

I know it because I read it in the papers. I also know it to be the case because in every country I have graced with my presence up to the present time, or have heard from, the possessing classes through their organs in the press, and their spokesmen upon the platform have been vociferous and insistent in declaring the foreign origin of Socialism.

In Ireland Socialism is an English importation, in England they are convinced it was made in Germany, in Germany it is a scheme of traitors in alliance with the French to disrupt the Empire, in France it is an accursed conspiracy to discredit the army which is destined to reconquer Alsace and Lorraine, in Russia it is an English plot to prevent Russian extension towards Asia, in Asia it is known to have been set on foot by American enemies of Chinese and Japanese industrial progress, and in America it is one of the baneful fruits of unrestricted pauper and criminal immigration.

All nations today repudiate Socialism, yet Socialist ideas are conquering all nations. When anything has to be done in a practical direction toward ameliorating the lot of the helpless ones, or towards using the collective force of society in strengthening the hands of the individual it is sure to be in the intellectual armory of Socialists the right weapon is found for the work.

A case in point. There are tens of thousands of hungry children in New York today as in every other large American city, and many well meant efforts have been made to succor them. Free lunches have been opened in the poorest districts, bread lines have been established and charitable organizations are busy visiting homes and schools to find out the worst cases. But all this has only touched the fringe of the destitution, with the additional aggravation that anything passing through the hands of these charitable committees usually costs ten times as much for administration as it bestows on the object of its charity.

Also that the investigation is usually more effectual in destroying the last vestiges of self-respect in its victims than in succoring their needs.

In the midst of this difficulty Superintendent Maxwell of the New York Schools sends a letter to a committee of thirteen charitable organizations which had met together to consider the problem, and in this letter he advocates the method of relieving distress long since initiated by the Socialist representatives in the Municipality of Paris. I quote from the New York World:

4

A committee of seven was appointed to inquire more fully into the question of feeding school children and to report at a subsequent meeting. School Superintendent Maxwell sent a letter advocating the establishment in New York schools with city money of lunch kitchens, these to sell food at actual cost and to give to needy children tickets just like those paid for, to the end that no child might know that his fellow was eating at the expense of the city by the color of his ticket. This is done in Paris.

Contrast this solicitude for the self-respect of the poor children, recognized by Superintendent Maxwell in the plan of these 'foreign Socialists' with the insulting methods of the capitalist 'bread lines' and charitable organizations in general.

But all the same it is too horrible to take practical examples in relieving the distress caused by capitalist society from pestilent agitators who wish to destroy the society whose victims they are succoring, and mere foreigners, too. The capitalist method of parading mothers and children for an hour in the street before feeding them is more calculated to build up the proper degree of pride in the embryo American citizens; and make them appreciate the benefits their fathers and brothers are asked to vote for.

Read this telling how hungry children and mothers

stood patiently waiting for a meal on the sidewalk, and whoop it up for pure ecstasy of joy that you are permitted to live in a system of society wherein a great metropolitan daily thought that the fact of five hundred children getting a 'hearty luncheon' was remarkable enough to deserve a paragraph:

> Five hundred ill-fed children who attend the schools on the lower east side got a hearty luncheon yesterday when the first of the children's lunchrooms was opened at Canal and Forsyth streets. Long before noon there was a large gathering of children, some of them accompanied by their mothers, awaiting the opening of the doors.

WELL, I AM NOT INTERESTED IN INTERNATIONALISM. THIS COUNTRY IS GOOD ENOUGH FOR ME.

Is that so? Say: Are you taking a share in the Moscow-Windau-Rydinsk Railway?

'No, where is that?'

My dear friend, where that railway runs has nothing to do with you. What you have to do is simply to take a share, and then go and have a good time whilst the Russian railway workers, whom you do not know, working in a country you never saw, speaking a language you don't understand, earn your dividends by the sweat of their brows.

Curious, ain't it?

We Socialists are always talking about the international solidarity of labor, about the oneness of our interests all over the world, and ever and anon working off our heaving chests a peroration on the bonds of fraternal sympathy which should unite the wage slaves of the capitalist system.

But there is another kind of bond - Russian railway bonds - which join, not the workers, but the idlers of the world in fraternal sympathy, and which creates among the members of the capitalist class a feeling of identity of interest, of international solidarity, which they don't perorate about but which is most potent and effective notwithstanding.

You do not fully recognize the fact that the internationality of Socialism is at most but a lame and halting attempt to create a counterpoise to the internationality of capitalism. Yet so it is.

Here is a case in point. The Moscow-Windau-Rydinsk railway is, as its name indicates, a railway running, or proposed to be run, from one part of Russia to another. You would think that that concerned the Russian people only, and that our patriotic capitalist class, always so ready to declare against working class Socialists with international sympathies, would never look at it or touch it.

You would not think that Ireland, for example - whose professional patriots are forever telling the gullible working men that Ireland will be ruined for the lack of capital and enterprise - would be a good country to find money in to finance a Russian railway.

Yet, observe the fact. All the Dublin papers of Monday, June 12, 1899, contained the prospectus of this far away Russian railway, offered for the investment of Irish capitalists, and offered by a firm of London stockbrokers who are astute enough not to waste money in endeavoring to catch fish in waters where they were not in the habit of biting freely.

And in the midst of the Russian revolution the agents of the Czar succeeded in obtaining almost unlimited treasures in the United States to pay the expenses of throttling the infant Liberty.

As the shares in Russian railways were sold in Ireland, as Russian bonds were sold in America, so the shares in American mines, railroads and factories are bought and sold on all the stock exchanges of Europe and Asia by men who never saw America in their lifetime.

Now, let us examine the situation, keeping in mind the fact that this is but a type of what prevails all round; you can satisfy yourself on that head by a daily glance at our capitalist papers.

CAPITAL IS INTERNATIONAL

The shares of Russian railways, African mines, Nicaraguan canals, Chilian gas works, Norwegian timber, Mexican water works, Canadian fur trappings, Australian kanaka slave trade, Indian tea plantations, Japanese linen factories, Chinese cotton mills, European national and municipal debts, United States bonanza farms are bought and sold every day by investors, many of whom never saw any one of the countries in which their money is invested, but who have, by virtue of so investing, a legal right to a share of the plunder extracted under the capitalist system from the wage workers whose bone and sinew earn the dividends upon the bonds they have purchased.

When our investing classes purchase a share in any capitalist concern, in any country whatsoever, they do so, not in order to build up a useful industry, but because the act of purchase endows them with a prospective share of the spoils it is proposed to wring from labor.

Therefore, every member of the investing classes is interested to the extent of his investments, present or prospective, in the subjection of Labor all over the world.

That is the internationality of Capital and Capitalism.

The wage worker is oppressed under this system in the interest of a class of capitalist investors who may be living thousands of miles away and whose very names are unknown to him.

He is, therefore, interested in every revolt of Labor all over the world, for the very individuals against whom that revolt may be directed may - by the wondrous mechanism of the capitalist system - through shares, bonds, national and municipal debts

- be the parasites who are sucking his blood also. That is one of the underlying facts inspiring the internationalism of Labor and Socialism.

[OLD AGE PENSIONS]

BUT THE SOCIALIST PROPOSALS, THEY SAY, WOULD DESTROY THE INDIVIDUAL CHARACTER OF THE WORKER. HE WOULD LEAN ON THE COMMUNITY, INSTEAD OF UPON HIS OWN EFFORTS.

Yes: Giving evidence before the Old Age Pensions Committee in England, Sir John Dorrington, M.P., expressed the belief that the provision of Old Age Pensions by the State, for instance, would do more harm than good. It was an objectionable principle, and would lead to improvidence.'

There now! You will always observe that it is some member of what an Irish revolutionist called 'the canting, fed classes', who is anxious that nothing should be done by the State to give the working class habits of 'improvidence,' or to do us any 'harm.' Dear, kind souls!

To do them justice they are most consistent. For both in public and private their efforts are most whole-heartedly bent in the same direction, viz., to prevent improvidence - ON OUR PART.

They lower our wages - to prevent improvidence; they increase our rents - to prevent improvidence; they periodically suspend us from our employment - to prevent improvidence, and as soon as we are worn out in their service they send us to a semi-convict establishment, known as the Workhouse, where we are scientifically starved to death - to prevent improvidence.

Old Age Pensions might do us harm. Ah, yes! And yet, come to think of it, I know quite a number of people who draw Old Age Pensions and it doesn't do them a bit of harm. Strange, isn't it?

Then all the Royal Families have pensions, and they don't seem to do them any harm; royal babies, in fact, begin to draw pensions and milk from a bottle at the same time.

Afterwards they drop the milk, but they never drop the pension - nor the bottle.

Then all our judges get pensions, and are not corrupted thereby - at least not more than usual. In fact, all well-paid officials in governmental or municipal service get pensions, and there are no fears expressed that the receipt of the same may do them harm.

But the underpaid, overworked wage-slave. To give him a pension would ruin his moral fibre, weaken his stamina, debase his manhood, sap his integrity, corrupt his morals, check his prudence, emasculate his character, lower his aspirations, vitiate his resolves, destroy his self-reliance, annihilate his rectitude, corrode his virility - and - and - other things.

[PRACTICAL POLITICS]

LET US BE PRACTICAL. WE WANT
SOMETHING PR-R-RACTICAL.

Always the cry of hum-drum mediocrity, afraid to
face the stern necessity for uncompromising action.
That saying has done more yeoman service in the
cause of oppression than all its avowed supporters.

The average man dislikes to be thought unpractical,
and so, while frequently loathing the principles or
distrusting the leaders of the particular political
party he is associated with, declines to leave them,
in the hope that their very lack of earnestness may
be more fruitful of practical results than the honest
outspokenness of the party in whose principles he
does believe.

In the phraseology of politics, a party too
indifferent to the sorrow and sufferings of humanity
to raise its voice in protest, is a moderate, practical
party; whilst a party totally indifferent to the
personality of leaders, or questions of leadership,
but hot to enthusiasm on every question affecting
the well-being of the toiling masses, is an extreme,
a dangerous party.

Yet, although it may seem a paradox to say so,
there is no party so incapable of achieving practical
results as an orthodox political party; and there is
no party so certain of placing moderate reforms to
its credit as an extreme - a revolutionary party.

The possessing classes will and do laugh to scorn

every scheme for the amelioration of the workers so long as those responsible for the initiation of the scheme admit as justifiable the 'rights of property'; but when the public attention is directed towards questioning the justifiable nature of those 'rights' in themselves, then the master class, alarmed for the safety of their booty, yield reform after reform - in order to prevent revolution.

Moral - Don't be 'practical' in politics. To be practical in that sense means that you have schooled yourself to think along the lines, and in the grooves those who rob you would desire you to think.

In any case it is time we got rid of all the cant about 'politics' and 'constitutional agitation' in general. For there is really no meaning whatever in those phrases.

Every public question is a political question. The men who tell us that Labor questions, for instance, have nothing to do with politics, understand neither the one nor the other. The Labor question cannot be settled except by measures which necessitate a revision of the whole system of society, which, of course, implies political warfare to secure the power to effect such revision.

If by politics we understand the fight between the outs and ins, or the contest for party leadership, then Labor is rightly supremely indifferent to such politics, but to the politics which center round the question of property and the administration thereof Labor is not, cannot be, indifferent.

To effect its emancipation Labor must reorganize society on the basis of labor; this cannot be done while the forces of government are in the hands of the rich, therefore the governing power must be wrested from the hands of the rich peaceably if possible, forcibly if necessary.

In the phraseology of the master class and its pressmen the trade unionist who is not a Socialist is more practical than he who is, and the worker who is neither one nor the other but can resign himself to the state of slavery in which he was born, is the most practical of all men.

The heroes and martyrs who in the past gave up their lives for the liberty of the race were not practical, but they were heroes all the same.

The slavish multitude who refused to second their efforts from a craven fear lest their skins might suffer were practical, but they were soulless serfs, nevertheless.

Revolution is never practical - until the hour of the Revolution strikes. Then it alone is practical, and all the efforts of the conservatives and compromisers become the most futile and visionary of human imaginings.

For that hour let us work, think and hope; for that hour let us pawn our present ease in hopes of a glorious redemption; for that hour let us prepare the hosts of Labor with intelligence sufficient to laugh at the nostrums dubbed practical by our slave-lords, practical for the perpetuation of our slavery; for

14

that supreme crisis of human history let us watch, like sentinels, with weapons ever ready, remembering always that there can be no dignity in Labor until Labor knows no master.

[CONFISCATION]

WOULD YOU CONFISCATE THE PROPERTY OF THE CAPITALIST CLASS AND ROB MEN OF THAT WHICH THEY HAVE, PERHAPS, WORKED A WHOLE LIFETIME TO ACCUMULATE?

Yes, sir, and certainly not.

We would certainly confiscate the property of the capitalist class, but we do not propose to rob anyone. On the contrary, we propose to establish honesty once and forever as the basis of our social relations. This Socialist movement is indeed worthy to be entitled The Great Anti-Theft Movement of the Twentieth Century.

You see, confiscation is one great certainty of the future for every business man outside of the trust. It lies with him to say if it will be confiscation by the Trust in the interest of the Trust, or confiscation by Socialism in the interest of All.

If he resolves to continue to support the capitalist order of society he will surely have his property confiscated. After having, as you say, 'worked for a whole lifetime to accumulate' a fortune, to establish a business on what he imagined would be a sound foundation, on some fine day the Trust will enter into competition with him, will invade his market, use their enormous capital to undersell him at ruinous prices, take his customers from him, ruin his business, and finally drive him into bankruptcy, and perhaps to end his days as a pauper.

That is capitalist confiscation! It is going on all around us, and every time the business man who is not a Trust Magnate votes for capitalism, he is working to prepare that fate for himself.

On the other hand, if he works for Socialism it also will confiscate his property. But it will only do so in order to acquire the industrial equipment necessary to establish a system of society in which the whole human race will be secured against the fear of want for all time, a System in which all men and women will be joint heirs and owners of all the intellectual and material conquests made possible by associated effort.

Socialism will confiscate the property of the capitalist and in return will secure the individual against poverty and oppres- sion; it, in return for so confiscating, will assure to all men and women a free, happy and unanxious human life. And that is more than capitalism can assure anyone today.

So you see the average capitalist has to choose between two kinds of confiscation. One or the other he must certainly endure. Confiscation by the Trust and consequently bankruptcy, poverty and perhaps pauperism in his old age, or

Confiscation by Socialism and consequently

security, plenty and a Care-Free Life to him and his to the remotest generation.

Which will it be?

BUT IT IS THEIR PROPERTY. WHY SHOULD SOCIALISTS CONFISCATE IT?

Their property, eh? Let us see: Here is a cutting from the New York World giving a synopsis of the Annual Report of the Coats Thread Company of Pawtucket, Rhode Island, for 1907. Now, let us examine it, and bear in mind that this company is the basis of the Thread Trust, with branches in Paisley, Scotland, and on the continent of Europe.

Also bear in mind that it is not a 'horrible example', but simply a normal type of a normally conducted industry, and therefore what applies to it will apply in a greater or less degree to all others.

This report gives the dividend for the year at 20 per cent per annum. Twenty per cent dividend means 20 cents on the dollar profit. Now, what is a profit?

According to Socialists, profit only exists when all other items of production are paid for. The workers by their labor must create enough wealth to pay for certain items before profit appears. They must pay for the cost of raw material, the wear and tear of machinery, buildings, etc. (the depreciation of capital), the wages of superintendence, their own wages, and a certain amount to be left aside as a reserve fund to meet all possible contingencies. After, and only after, all these items have been paid for by their labor, all that is left is profit.

With this company the profit amounted to 20 cents on every dollar invested.

What does this mean? It means that in the course of five years - five times 20 cents equals one dollar - the workers in the industry had created enough profit to buy the whole industry from its present owners. It means that after paying all the expenses of the factory, including their own wages, they created enough profit to buy the whole building, from the roof to the basement, all the offices and agencies, and everything in the shape of capital. All this in five years.

And after they had so bought it from the capitalists it still belonged to the capitalists.

It means that if a capitalist had invested $1,000 in that industry, in the course of five years he would draw out a thousand dollars, and still have a thousand dollars lying there untouched; in the course of ten years, he would draw two thousand dollars, in fifteen years he would draw three thousand dollars. And still his first thousand dollars would be as virgin as ever.

You understand that this has been going on ever since the capitalist system came into being; all the capital in the world has been paid for by the working class over and over again, and we are still creating it, and recreating it. And the oftener we buy it the less it belongs to us.

The capital of the master class is not their property; it is the unpaid labor of the working class - 'the hire of the laborer kept back by fraud'.

[HOLIDAYS]

OH, THE CAPITALIST HAS HIS ANXIETIES, TOO. AND THE WORKER HAS OFTEN A GOOD TIME.

Sure: Say, where were you for the holidays?

Were you tempted to go abroad? Did you visit Europe? Did you riot, in all the abandonment of a wage slave let loose, among the pleasure haunts of the world?

Perhaps you went to the Riviera; perhaps you luxuriated in ecstatic worship of that glorious bit of Nature's handiwork where the blue waters of the Mediterranean roll in all their entrancing splendor against the shores of classic Italy.

Perhaps you rambled among the vine clad hills of sunny France, and visited the spots hallowed by the hand of that country's glorious history.

Perhaps you sailed up the castellated Rhine, toasted the eyes of bewitching German frauleins in frothy German beer, explored the recesses of the legend haunted Hartz mountains, and established a nodding acquaintance with the Spirit of the Brocken.

Perhaps you traversed the lakes and fjords of Norway, sat down in awe before the neglected magnificence of the Alhambra, had a cup of coffee with Menelik of Abyssinia, smelt afar off the odors of the streets of Morocco, climbed the Pyramids of Egypt, shared the hospitable tent of the Bedouin, visited Cyprus, looked in at Constantinople, ogled the dark- eyed beauties of Circassia, rubbed up against the Cossack in his Ural mountains, or

Perhaps you lay in bed all day in order to save a meal, and listened to your wife wondering how she could make ends meet with a day's pay short in the weekly wages.

And whilst you thus squandered your substance in riotous living, did you ever stop to think of your master - your poor, dear, overworked, tired master?

Did you ever stop to reflect upon the pitiable condition of that individual who so kindly provides you with employment, and does no useful work himself in order that you may get plenty of it?

When you consider how hard a task it was for you to decide in what manner you should spend your Holiday; where you should go for that ONE DAY, then you must perceive how hard it is for your masters to find a way in which to spend the practically perpetual holiday which you force upon them by your love for work.

Ah, yes, that large section of our masters who have realized that ideal of complete idleness after which all our masters strive, those men who do not work, never did work, and with the help of God - and the ignorance of the people - never intend to work, how terrible must be their lot in life!

We, who toil from early morn till late at night, from

January till December, from childhood to old age, have no care or trouble or mental anxiety to cross our mind - except the landlord, the fear of loss of employment, the danger of sickness, the lack of common necessities, to say nothing of luxuries, for our children, the insolence of our superiors, the unhealthy condition of our homes, the exhausting nature of our toil, the lack of all opportunities of mental cultivation, and the ever present question whether we shall shuffle off this mortal coil in a miserable garret, be killed by hard work, or die in the Poorhouse.

With these trifling exceptions we have nothing to bother us; but the boss, ah, the poor, poor boss!

He has everything to bother him. Whilst we are amusing ourselves in the hold of a ship shoveling coal, swinging a hammer in front of a forge, toiling up a ladder with bricks, stitching until our eyes grow dim at the board, gaily riding up and down for twelve hours per day, seven days per week, on a trolley car, riding around the city in all weather with teams or swinging by the skin of our teeth on the iron framework of a skyscraper, standing at our ease OUTSIDE the printing office door listening to the musical click of the linotype as it performs the work we used to do INSIDE, telling each other comforting stories about the new machinery which takes our places as carpenters, harness-makers, tinplate-workers, laborers, etc., in short whilst we are enjoying our- selves, free from all mental worry.

Our unselfish tired-out bosses are sitting at home, with their feet on the table, softly patting the bottom button of their vests.

Working with their brains.

Poor bosses! Mighty brains!

Without our toil they would never get the education necessary to develop their brains; if we were not defrauded by their class of the fruits of our toil we could provide for education enough to develop the mental powers of all, and so deprive the ruling class of the last vestige of an excuse for clinging to mastership, viz., their assumed intellectual superiority.

I say 'assumed', because the greater part of the brain- work of industry today is performed by men taken from the ranks of the workers, and paid high salaries in proportion as they develop expertness as slave-drivers.

As education spreads among the people the workers will want to enjoy life more; they will assert their right to the full fruits of their labor, and by that act of self-assertion lay the foundation of that Socialist Republic in which the labor will be so easy, and the reward so great, that life will seem a perpetual holiday.

BUT SOCIALISM IS AGAINST RELIGION. I CAN'T BE A SOCIALIST AND BE A CHRISTIAN.

O, quit your fooling! That talk is all right for those

who know nothing of the relations between capital and labor, or are innocent of any knowledge of the processes of modern industry, or imagine that men, in their daily struggles for bread or fortunes, are governed by the Sermon on the Mount.

But between workingmen that talk is absurd. We know that Socialism bears upon our daily life in the workshop, and that religion does not; we know that the man who never set foot in a church in his lifetime will, if he is rich, be more honored by Christian society than the poor man who goes to church every Sunday, and says his prayers morning and evening; we know that the capitalists of all religions pay more for the service of a good lawyer to keep them out of the clutches of the law than for the services of a good priest to keep them out of the clutches of the devil; and we never heard of a capitalist, who, in his business, respected the Sermon on the Mount as much as he did the decisions of the Supreme Court.

These things we know. We also know that neither capitalist nor worker can practice the moral precepts of religion, and without its moral precepts a religion is simply a sham. If a religion cannot enforce its moral teachings upon its votaries it has as little relation to actual life as the pre-election promises of a politician have to legislation.

We know that Christianity teaches us to love our neighbor as ourselves, but we also know that if a capitalist attempted to run his business upon that plan his relatives would have no difficulty in getting lawyers, judges and physicians to declare him incompetent to conduct his affairs in the business world.

He would not be half as certain of reaching Heaven in the next world as he would be of getting into the 'bughouse' in this.

And, as for the worker. Well, in the fall of 1908, the New York World printed an advertisement for a teamster in Brooklyn, wages to be $12 per week. Over 700 applicants responded. Now, could each of these men love their neighbors in that line of hungry competitors for that pitiful wage?

As each man stood in line in that awful parade of misery could he pray for his neighbor to get the job, and could he be expected to follow up his prayer by giving up his chance, and so making certain the prolongation of the misery of his wife and little ones?

No, my friend, Socialism is a bread and butter question. It is a question of the stomach; it is going to be settled in the factories, mines and ballot boxes of this country and is not going to be settled at the altar or in the church.

This is what our well-fed friends call a 'base, material standpoint', but remember that beauty, and genius and art and poetry and all the finer efflorescences of the higher nature of man can only be realized in all their completeness upon the material basis of a healthy body, that not only an army but the whole human race marches upon its stomach, and then you will grasp the full wisdom of our position.

That the question to be settled by Socialism is the effect of private ownership of the means of production upon the well-being of the race; that we are determined to have a straight fight upon the question between those who believe that such private ownership is destructive of human well-being and those who believe it to be beneficial, that as men of all religions and of none are in the ranks of the capitalists, and men of all religions and of none are on the side of the workers the attempt to make religion an issue in the question is an intrusion, an impertinence and an absurdity.

Personally I am opposed to any system wherein the capitalist is more powerful than God Almighty. You need not serve God unless you like, and may refuse to serve him and grow fat, prosperous and universally respected. But if you refuse to serve the capitalist your doom is sealed; misery and poverty and public odium await you.

No worker is compelled to enter a church and to serve God; every worker is compelled to enter the employment of a capitalist and serve him.

As Socialists we are concerned to free mankind from the servitude forced upon them as a necessity of their life; we propose to allow the question of all kinds of service voluntarily rendered to be settled by the emancipated human race of the future.

I do not deny that Socialists often leave the church.

But why do they do so? Is their defection from the church a result of our attitude towards religion; or is it the result of the attitude of the church and its ministers toward Socialism?

Let us take a case in point, one of those cases that are being paralleled every day in our midst. An Irish Catholic joins the Socialist movement. He finds that as a rule the Socialist men and women are better educated than their fellows; he finds that they are immensely cleaner in speech and thought than are the adherents of capitalism in the same class; that they are devoted husbands and loyal wives, loving and cheerful fathers and mothers, skilful and industrious workers in the shops and office, and that although poor and needy as a rule, yet that they continually bleed themselves to support their cause, and give up for Socialism what many others spend in the saloon.

He finds that a drunken Socialist is as rare as a white black-bird, and that a Socialist of criminal tendencies is such a rara avis that when one is found the public press heralds it forth as a great discovery.

Democratic and republican jailbirds are so common that the public press do not regard their existence as 'news' to anybody, nor yet does the public press think it necessary to say that certain criminals belong to the Protestant or Catholic religions. That is nothing unusual, and therefore not worth printing. But a criminal Socialist - that would be news indeed!

Our Irish Catholic Socialist gradually begins to notice these things. He looks around and he finds the press full of reports of crimes, murders, robberies, bank swindlers, forgeries, debauches, gambling transactions, and midnight orgies in which the most revolting indecencies are perpetrated. He investigates and he discovers that the perpetrators of these crimes were respectable capitalists, pillars of society, and red-hot enemies of Socialism, and that the dives in which the highest and the lowest meet together in a saturnalia of vice contribute a large proportion of the campaign funds of the capitalist political parties.

Some Sunday he goes to Mass as usual, and he finds that at Gospel the priest launches out into a political speech and tells the congregation that the honest, self-sacrificing, industrious, clean men and women, whom he calls 'comrades,' are a wicked, impious, dissolute sect, desiring to destroy the home, to distribute the earnings of the provident among the idle and lazy of the world, and reveling in all sorts of impure thoughts about women.

And as this Irish Catholic Socialist listens to this foul libel, what wonder if the hot blood of anger rushes to his face, and he begins to believe that the temple of God has itself been sold to the all desecrating grasp of the capitalist?

While he is yet wondering what to think of the matter, he hears that his immortal soul will be lost if he fails to vote for capitalism, and he reflects that if he lined up with the brothel keepers, gambling house proprietors, race track swindlers, and white slave traders to vote the capitalist ticket, this same priest would tell him he was a good Catholic and loyal son of the church.

At such a juncture the Irish Catholic Socialist often rises up, goes out of the church and wipes its dust off his feet forever. Then we are told that Socialism took him away from the church. But did it? Was it not rather the horrible spectacle of a priest of God standing up in the Holy Presence lying about and slandering honest men and women, and helping to support political parties whose campaign fund in every large city represents more bestiality than ever Sodom and Gomorrah knew?

These are the things that drive Socialists from the church, and the responsibility for every soul so lost lies upon those slanderers and not upon the Socialist movement.

[SOCIALISM AND NATIONALISM]

WELL, YOU WON'T GET THE IRISH TO HELP YOU. OUR IRISH-AMERICAN LEADERS TELL US THAT ALL WE IRISH IN THIS COUNTRY OUGHT TO STAND TOGETHER AND USE OUR VOTES TO FREE IRELAND.

Sure, let us free Ireland!

Never mind such base, carnal thoughts as concern work and wages, healthy homes, or lives unclouded by poverty.

Let us free Ireland!

The rackrenting landlord; is he not also an Irishman, and wherefore should we hate him? Nay, let us not speak harshly of our brother - yea, even when he raises our rent.

Let us free Ireland!

The profit-grinding capitalist, who robs us of three-fourths of the fruits of our labor, who sucks the very marrow of our bones when we are young, and then throws us out in the street, like a worn-out tool, when we are grown prematurely old in his service, is he not an Irishman, and mayhap a patriot, and wherefore should we think harshly of him?

Let us free Ireland!

'The land that bred and bore us.' And the landlord who makes us pay for permission to live upon it.

Whoop it up for liberty!

'Let us free Ireland,' says the patriot who won't touch Socialism.

Let us all join together and cr-r-rush the br-r-rutal Saxon. Let us all join together, says he, all classes and creeds.

And, says the town worker, after we have crushed the Saxon and freed Ireland, what will we do?

Oh, then you can go back to your slums, same as before.

Whoop it up for liberty!

And, says the agricultural workers, after we have

freed Ireland, what then?

Oh, then you can go scraping around for the landlord's rent or the money-lenders' interest same as before.

Whoop it up for liberty!

After Ireland is free, says the patriot who won't touch Socialism, we will protect all classes, and if you won't pay your rent you will be evicted same as now. But the evicting party, under command of the sheriff, will wear green uniforms and the Harp without the Crown, and the warrant turning you out on the roadside will be stamped with the arms of the Irish Republic.

Now, isn't that worth fighting for?

And when you cannot find employment, and, giving up the struggle of life in despair, enter the Poorhouse, the band of the nearest regiment of the Irish army will escort you to the Poorhouse door to the tune of 'St. Patrick's Day'.

Oh, it will be nice to live in those days!

'With the Green Flag floating o'er us' and an ever-increasing army of unemployed workers walking about under the Green Flag, wishing they had something to eat. Same as now!

Whoop it up for liberty!

Now, my friend, I also am Irish, but I'm a bit more logical. The capitalist, I say, is a parasite on industry; as useless in the present stage of our industrial development as any other parasite in the animal or vegetable world is to the life of the animal or vegetable upon which it feeds.

The working class is the victim of this parasite - this human leech, and it is the duty and interest of the working class to use every means in its power to oust this parasite class from the position which enables it to thus prey upon the vitals of Labor.

Therefore, I say, let us organize as a class to meet our masters and destroy their mastership; organize to drive them from their hold upon public life through their political power; organize to wrench from their robber clutch the land and workshops on and in which they enslave us; organize to cleanse our social life from the stain of social cannibalism, from the preying of man upon his fellow man.

Organize for a full, free and happy life FOR ALL OR FOR NONE.

SECTION II - POLITICAL ACTION OF LABOR

The great strike of the shop employes

on the Canadian Pacific Railway has been declared off - lost. While the shopmen were fighting desperately to maintain their organization and decent working conditions, the engineers, firemen, conductors, trainmen, etc., worked with scabs imported from the states and from Europe, and thus by keeping trains moving aided to break the strike. It is only one more illustration of what a vicious, not to say downright criminal, scheme craft autonomy actually is in practice.

Here's another example: After four years of hard fighting from the Mississippi river to the Pacific coast and from the Ohio river to the gulf, the machinists have been compelled to abandon their strikes on the Santa Fe and the L. & N. railways. The engines and cars built and repaired in the railway shops by strike-breakers were hauled over the roads by members of the old brotherhoods without the slightest objections. No wonder that onlookers become disgusted with such unionism.' Some union cards cover a multitude of sins.

MAX HAYES in *International Socialist Review*

INDUSTRIAL AND POLITICAL UNITY

At meetings throughout this country one frequently hears speakers laboring to arouse the workers to their duty, exclaim- ing:

> 'You unite industrially, why then do you divide politically? You unite against the bosses in strikes and lock-outs, and then you foolishly divide when you go to the ballot-box. Why not unite at the ballot-box as you unite in the workshop? Why not show the same unity on the political field as you do on the industrial battlefield?'

At first blush this looks to be an exceedingly apt and forcible form of appeal to our fellow-workers, but when examined more attentively it will be seen that in view of the facts of our industrial warfare this appeal is based upon a flagrant mis-statement of facts. The real truth is that the workers do not unite industrially, but on the contrary are most hopelessly divided on the industrial field, and that their division and confusion on the political field are the direct result of their division and confusion on the industrial field. It would be easy to prove that even our most loyal trade unionists habitually play the game of the capitalist class on the industrial field just as surely as the Republican and Democratic workers do it on the political field. Let us examine the situation on the industrial field and see if it justifies the claim that economically the workers are united, or if it justifies the contention I make that the division of the workers on the political field is but the reflex of the confused ideas derived from the practice of the workers in strikes and lock-outs.

Quite recently we had a great strike of the workers employed on the Subway and Elevated Systems of street car service in New York. The men showed a splendid front against the power of the mammoth capitalist company headed by August Belmont, against which they were arrayed. Conductors, motormen, ticket-choppers, platform men, repairers, permanent way men, ticket-sellers - all went out together and for a time paralyzed the entire traffic on their respective system. The company, on the other hand, had the usual recourse to Jim Farley and his scabs and sought to man the trains with those professional traitors to their class. The number of scabs was large, but small in proportion to the men on strike, yet the strike was broken. It was not the scabs, however, who turned the scale against the strikers in favor of the men. That service to capital was performed by good union men with union cards in their pockets. These men were the engineers in the power houses which supplied the electric power to run the cars, and without whom all the scabs combined could not have run a single trip. A scab is a vile creature, but what shall we say of the men who helped the scab to commit his act of treason? The law says that an accessory before the fact is equally guilty of a crime with the actual criminal. What, then, are the trade unionists who supplied the power to scabs to help them break a strike?

They were unconsciously being compelled by their false system of organization to betray their struggling brothers. Was this unity on the industrial field? And is it any wonder that the men accustomed to so scab upon their fellow-workers in a lab or struggle should also scab it upon their class in a political struggle? Is it not rather common sense to expect that the recognition of the necessity for concerted common action of all workers against the capitalist enemy in the industrial battle ground must precede the realization of the wisdom of common action as a class on the political battlefield? The men who are taught that it is all right to continue working for a capitalist against whom their shop-mates of a different craft are on strike are not likely to see any harm in continuing to vote for a capitalist nominee at the polls even when he is opposed by the candidate of a Labor organization. Political scabbery is born of industrial scabbery; it is its legitimate offspring.

Instances of this industrial disunion could be cited in- definitely. The Longshoremen of the Port of New York went out on strike. They at first succeeded in tying up the ships of the Shipping Trust, great as its wealth is, and in demonstrating the real power of labor when unhampered by contracts with capital. The Shipping Trust was taken by surprise, but quickly recovered, and as usual imported scabs from all over the country.

Then was seen what the unity of the working class on the industrial field amounts to under present conditions. As scab longshoremen unloaded the ship, union teamsters with union buttons in their hats received the goods from their hands, loaded them into their wagons, and drove merrily away.

As scab longshoremen loaded a ship union men coaled it, and when the cargo was safely on board union marine engineers set up steam, and union seamen and firemen took it out of the dock on its voyage to its destination. Can men who are trained and taught to believe that such a course of conduct is right and proper be expected to realize the oneness of the interests of the working class as a whole against the capitalist class as a whole, and vote and act accordingly? In short, can their field of vision be so extensive that it can see the brotherhood of all men, and yet so restricted that it can see no harm in a brother labor organization in their own industry being beaten to death by capital?

Contrast this woeful picture of divided and disorganized 'unionism' in America with the following account from the New York Sun of the manner in which the Socialist unionists of Scandinavia stand together in a fight against the common enemy, irrespective of 'craft interests' or 'craft contracts':

> A short sojourn in Scandinavia, particularly in Copenhagen and the southern part of Sweden, gives one an

object lesson in socialism. In some way or other the socialists have managed to capture all the trade unions in these parts and between them have caused a reign of terror for everybody who is unfortunate enough to own a business of any sort. Heaven help him if he fires one of his helps or tries to assert himself in any way. He is immediately declared in 'blockade'.

This socialist term means practically the same as a boycott. If the offending business man happens to be a retail merchant all workmen are warned off his premises. The drivers for the wholesale houses refuse to deliver goods at his store; the truckmen refuse to cart anything to or from his place, and so on; in fact, he is a doomed man unless he comes to terms with the union. It is worth mentioning that boycotting bulletins and also the names and addresses of those who are bold enough to help the man out are published in leaded type in all the socialistic newspapers. A law to prevent the publication of such boycotting announcements was proposed in the Swedish riksdag this year, but was defeated.

If the boycotted person be a wholesale dealer the proceedings are much the same, or, rather, they are reversed. The retailers are threatened with the loss of the workmen's trade unless they cease dealing with such a firm; the truckmen refuse to haul for it. It has even happened that the scavengers have refused to remove the refuse from the premises. More often, however, the cans are 'accidentally' dropped on the stairs. These scavengers belong to the cities' own forces, as a rule, and receive pensions after a certain length of service, but they have all sworn allegiance to the socialistic cause.

In reading the foregoing it is well to remember that practically all the workingmen of such cities - that is, practically all Sweden and Denmark - are union men, i.e., socialists, and are, therefore, able to carry out their threats.

Here we have a practical illustration of the power of Socialism when it rests upon an economic Organization, and the effectiveness and far-reaching activity of unionism when it is inspired by the Socialist ideal. Now as an equally valuable object lesson in American unionism, an object lesson in how not to do it, let us picture a typical state of affairs in the machine industry. The moulders' contract with the boss expires and they go out on strike. In a machine shop the moulder occupies a position intermediate between the pattern-maker and the machinist, or, as they are called in Ireland, the engineers. When the moulders go out the boss who has had all his plans laid for months beforehand brings in a staff of scabs and installs them in the places of the striking workers. Then the tragi-comedy begins. The union pattern-maker makes his patterns and hands them over to the scab moulder; the scab moulder casts his moulds and when they are done the union machinist takes them from him and placidly finishes the job. Then having finished their day's work, they go to their union meetings and vote donations of a few hundred dollars to help the strikers to defeat the boss, after they had worked all day to help the boss to defeat the strikers. Thus they exemplify the solidarity of labor. When the moulders are beaten the machinists and the pattemmakers, and the blacksmiths, and the electricians, and the engineers, and all the rest take their turn of going up against the boss in separate bodies to be licked. As each is taking its medicine its fellows of other crafts in the same shop sympathize with it in the name of the solidarity of labor, and continue to work in the service of the capitalist, against whom the strike is directed, in the name of the sacred contract of the craft union.

When the coal miners of Pennsylvania had their famous strike in 1902 the railroad brotherhoods hauled in scabs to take their places, and when the scabs had mined coal the same railroad men hauled out this scab-mined coal.

Need I go on to prove the point that industrial division and discord is the order of the day amongst the workers, and that this disunion and confusion on the economic field cannot fail to perpetuate itself upon the political field? Those orators who reproach the workers with being divided on the political field, although united on the industrial, are simply mis-stating facts. The workers are divided on both, and as political parties are the reflex of economic conditions, it follows that industrial union once established will create the political unity of the working class. I feel that we cannot too strongly insist upon this point. Political division is born of industrial division; political scabbery is born of industrial craft scabbery; political weakness keeps even step with industrial weakness. It is an axiom enforced by all the experience of the ages that they who rule industrially will rule politically, and therefore they who are divided industrially will remain impotent politically. The failure of Mr. Gompers to unite politically the forces of the American Federation of Labor was the inevitable outcome of his own policy of division on the industrial battle ground; he reversed the natural process by trying to unite men on class lines whilst he opposed every effort, as in the case of the Brewers, to unite them on industrial lines. The natural lines of thought and action lead from the direct to the indirect, from the simple to the complex, from the immediate to the ultimate. Mr. Gompers ignored this natural line of development and preached the separation into craft organizations, with separate craft interests, of the workers, and then expected them to heed his call to unity on the less direct and immediate battleground of politics. He failed, as even the Socialists would fail if they remained equally blind to the natural law of our evolution into class consciousness. That natural law leads us as individuals to unite in our craft, as crafts to unite in our industry, as industries in our class, and the finished expression of that evolution is, we believe, the appearance of our class upon the political battle ground with all the economic power behind it to enforce its mandates. Until that day dawns our political parties of the working class are but propagandist agencies, John the Baptists of the New Redemption, but when that day dawns our political party will be armed with all the might of our class; will be revolutionary in fact as well as in thought.

To Irish men and women especially, I should not need to labour this point. The historic example of their Land League bequeaths to us a precious legacy of wisdom, both practical and revolutionary, outlining our proper course of action. During Land League days in Ireland when a tenant was evicted from a farm, not only his fellow-tenants but practically the whole country united to help him in his fight. When the evicted farm was rented by another tenant, a land-grabber or 'scab,' every person in the countryside shunned him as a leper, and, still better, fought him as a traitor. Nor did they make the mistake of fighting the traitor and yet working for his employer, the landlord. No, they included both in the one common hostility.

At the command of the Land League every servant

and laborer quit the service of the landlord. In Ireland, it is well to remember, in order to appreciate this act of the laborers, that the landlords were usually better paymasters and more generous employers than the tenant farmers. The laborers, therefore, might reasonably have argued that the fight of the tenant farmers was none of their business. But they indulged in no such blindly selfish hair-splitting. When the landlord had declared war upon the tenant by evicting him, the laborers responded by war upon the landlord. Servant boy and servant girl at once quit his service, the carman refused to drive him, the cook to cook for him, his linen remained unwashed, his harvest unreaped, his cows unmilked, his house and fields deserted. The grocer and the butcher, the physician and the schoolmaster were alike hostile to him; if the children of the land-grabber (scab) entered school all other children rose and left; if the land-grabber or his landlord attended Mass everyone else at Mass walked out in a body. They found it hard to get anyone to serve them or feed them in health, to attend them in sickness, or to bury those dear to them in death. It was this relentless and implacable war upon the landowning class and traitors among the tenant class which gave the word 'boycott' to the English language through its enforcement against an Irish landowner, Captain Boycott. It was often horrible, it was always ugly in appearance to the superficial observer, but it was marvelously effective. It put courage and hope and manhood into a class long reckoned as the most enslaved in Europe. It broke the back of the personal despotism of the Irish landlord and so crippled his social and economic power that Irish landed estates from being a favorite form of investment for the financial interests sank to such a position that even the most reckless moneylender would for a time scarce accept a mortgage upon them. That it failed of attaining real economic freedom for the Irish people was due not to any defect in its method of fighting, but rather to the fact that economic questions are not susceptible of being settled within the restricted radius of any one small nation, but are acted upon by influences world-wide in their character.

But how great a lesson for the American worker is to be found in this record of a class struggle in Ireland! The American worker was never yet so low in the social and political scale as the Irish tenant. Yet the Irish tenant rose and by sheer force of his unity on the economic field shattered the power of his master, whilst the American worker remaining divided upon the economic field sinks day by day lower toward serfdom. The Irish tenant had to contend against the overwhelming power of a foreign empire backing up the economic power of a native tyranny, yet he conquered, whilst the American worker able to become the political sovereign of the country remains the sport of the political factions of his masters and the slave of their social power.

The Irish tenant uniting on the economic field felt

his strength, and, carrying the fight into politics, simply swept into oblivion every individual or party that refused to serve his class interests, but the American toilers remain divided on the economic field, and hence are divided and impotent upon the political, zealous servants of every interest but their own.

Need I point the moral more? Every one who has the interests of the working class at heart, every one who wishes to see the Socialist Party command the allegiance of the political hosts of labor, should strive to realize industrial union as the solid foundation upon which alone the political unity of the workers can be built up and directed toward a revolutionary end. To this end all those who work for industrial unionism are truly co-operating even when they least care for political activities.

INDUSTRIAL UNIONISM AND CONSTRUCTIVE SOCIALISM

There is not a socialist in the world today who can indicate with any degree of clearness how we can bring about the co-operative commonwealth except along the lines suggested by industrial organization of the workers.

Political institutions are not adapted to the administration of industry. Only industrial organizations are adapted to the administration of a co-operative commonwealth that we are working for. Only the industrial form of organization offers us even a theoretical constructive socialist program. There is no constructive socialism except in the industrial field.

The above extract from the speech of a delegate to the National Convention of the Socialist Party, Delegate Stirton, Editor of the Wage Slave, of Hancock, Michigan, so well embodies my ideas upon this matter that I have thought well to take them as a text for an article in explanation of the structural form of Socialist Society. In a previous chapter I have analyzed the weakness of the craft or trade union form of organization alike as a weapon of defense against the capitalist class in the everyday conflicts on the economic field, and as a generator of class consciousness on the political field, and pointed out the greater effectiveness for both purposes of an industrial form of organization. In the present article I desire to show how they who are engaged in building up industrial organizations for the practical purposes of today are at the same time preparing the framework of the society of the future. It is the realization of that fact that indeed marks the emergence of Socialism as a revolutionary force from the critical to the positive stage. Time was when Socialists, if asked how society would be organized under Socialism replied invariably, and airily, that such things would be left to the future to decide. The fact was that they had not considered the matter, but the development of the Trust and Organized Capital in general, making imperative the Industrial Organizations of Labor on similar lines has provided us with an answer at once more complete to ourselves and more satisfying to our questioners.

Now to analyze briefly the logical consequences of the position embodied in the above quotation.

> 'Political institutions are not adapted to
> the administration of industry.'

Here is a statement that no Socialist with a clear knowledge of the essentials of his doctrine can dispute. The political institutions of today are simply the coercive forces of capitalist society, they have grown up out of and are based upon territorial divisions of power in the hands of the ruling class in past ages, and were carried over into capitalist society to suit the needs of the capitalist class when that class overthrew the dominion of its predecessors. The delegation of the function of government into the hands of representatives elected from certain districts, states, or territories represents no real natural division suited to the requirements of modern society but is a survival from a time when territorial influences were more potent in the world than industrial influences, and for that reason is totally unsuited to the needs of the new social order which must be based upon industry. The Socialist thinker when he paints the structural form of the new social order does not imagine an industrial system directed or ruled by a body of men or women elected from an indiscriminate mass of residents within given districts, said residents working at a heterogeneous collection of trades and industries. To give the ruling, controlling and directing of industry into the hands of such a body would be too utterly foolish. What the Socialist does realize is that under a Social Democratic form of Society the administration of affairs will be in the hands of representatives of the various industries of the nation; that the workers in the shops and factories will organize themselves into unions, each union comprising all the workers at a given industry, that said union will democratically control the workshop life of its own industry, electing all foremen, etc., and regulating the routine of labor in that industry in subordination to the needs of society in general, to the needs of its allied trades and to the department of industry to which it belongs. That representatives elected from these various departments of industry will meet and form the industrial administration or national government of the country. In short Social Democracy, as its name implies, is the application to industry, or to the Social life of the nation, of the fundamental principles of democracy. Such application will necessarily have to begin in the workshop, and proceed logically and consecutively upward through all the grades of industrial Organization until it reaches the culminating point of national executive power and direction. In other words Social Democracy must proceed from the bottom upward, whereas capitalist political society is organized from above downward; Social Democracy will be administered by a committee of experts elected from the industries and professions of the land; capitalist society is governed by representatives elected from districts, and is based upon territorial division. The local and national governing or rather administrative bodies of Socialism will approach every question with impartial minds armed with the fullest expert knowledge born of experience; the governing bodies of capitalist society have to call in an expensive professional expert to instruct them on every technical question, and know that the impartiality of said expert varies with and depends upon the size of his fee.

It will be seen that this conception of Socialism destroys at one blow all the fears of a bureaucratic state, ruling and ordering the lives of every individual from above, and thus gives assurance that the social order of the future will be an extension of the freedom of the individual, and not a suppression of it. In short it blends the fullest democratic control with the most absolute expert supervision, something unthinkable of any society built upon the political state. To focus the idea properly in your mind you have but to realize how industry today transcends all limitations of territory and leaps across rivers, mountains and continents, then you can understand how impossible it would be to apply to such far reaching intricate enterprises the principle of democratic control by the workers through the medium of political territorial divisions.

Under Socialism states, territories or provinces will exist only as geographical expressions, and have no existence as sources of governmental power, though they may be seats of administrative bodies

Now having grasped the idea that the administrative force of the Socialist Republic of the future will function through unions industrially organized, that the principle of democratic control will operate through the workers correctly organized in such Industrial Unions, and that the political, territorial state of capitalist society will have no place or function under Socialism, you will at once grasp the full truth embodied in the words of this member of the Socialist Party whom I have just quoted, that 'only the industrial form of organization offers us even a theoretical constructive Socialist program.'

To some minds constructive Socialism is embodied in the work of our representatives on the various public bodies to which they have been elected. The various measures against the evils of capitalist property brought forward by, or as a result of the agitation of Socialist representatives on legislative bodies are figured as being of the nature of constructive Socialism. As we have shown the political state of capitalism has no place under Socialism, therefore measures which aim to place industries in the hands of or under the control of such a political state are in no sense steps towards that ideal; they are but useful measures to restrict the greed of capitalism and to familiarize the workers with the conception of common ownership. This latter is indeed their chief function. But the enrollment of the workers in unions patterned closely after the structure of modern industries, and following the organic lines of industrial development is par excellence the swiftest, safest, and most peaceful form of constructive work the Socialist can engage in. It prepares within the framework of capitalist society the working forms of the Socialist Republic, and thus while increasing the resisting power of the worker against present encroachments of the capitalist class it familiarizes him with the idea that the union he is helping to build up is destined to supplant that class in the control of the industry in which he is employed.

The power of this idea to transform the dry detail work of trade union organization into the constructive work of revolutionary Socialism, and thus to make of the unimaginative trade unionist a potent factor in the launching of a new system of society cannot be overestimated. It invests the sordid details of the daily incidents of the class struggle with a new and beautiful meaning, and presents them in their true light as skirmishes between the two opposing armies of light and darkness. In the light of this principle of Industrial Unionism every fresh shop or factory organized under its banner is a fort wrenched from the control of the capitalist class and manned with the soldiers of the Revolution to be held by them for the workers. On the day that the political and economic forces of labor finally break with capitalist society and proclaim the Workers Republic these shops and factories so manned by Industrial Unionists will be taken charge of by the workers there employed, and force and effectiveness thus given to that proclamation. Then and thus the new society will spring into existence ready equipped to perform all the useful functions of its predecessor.

THE FUTURE OF LABOR

In choosing for the subject of this chapter such a title as 'The Future of Labor,' I am aware that I run the risk of arousing expectations that I shall not be able to satisfy. The future of labor is a subject with which is bound up the future of civilization, and therefore a comprehensive treatment of the subject might be interpreted as demanding an analysis of all the forces and factors which will influence humanity in the future, and also their resultant effect.

Needless to say, my theme is a less ambitious one. I propose simply to deal with the problem of labor in the immediate future, with the marshalling of labor for the great conflict that confronts us, and with a consideration of the steps to be taken in order that the work of aiding the transition from Industrial Slavery to Industrial Freedom might be, as far as possible, freed from all encumbering and needless obstacles and expense of time, energy, and money.

But first and as an aid to a proper understanding of my position, let me place briefly before you my reading of the history of the past struggles of mankind against social subjection, my reading of the mental development undergone by each revolting class in the different stages of their struggle, from the first period of their bondage to the first dawn of their freedom. As I view it, such struggles had three well-marked mental stages, corresponding to the inception, development, and decay of the oppressing powers, and as I intend to attempt to apply this theory to the position of labor as a subject class today, I hope you will honor me by at least giving me your earnest attention to this conception, and aid by your discussion in determining at which of these periods or stages, the working class, the subject class of today, has arrived. My reading then briefly is this: That in the first period of bondage the eyes of the subject class are always turned toward the past, and all its efforts in revolt are directed to the end of destroying the social system in order that it might march backward and re-establish the social order of ancient times - 'the good old days.' That the goodness of those days was largely hypothetical seldom enters the imagination of men on whose limbs the fetters of oppression still sit awkwardly.

In the second period the subject class tends more and more to lose sight and recollection of any pre-existent state of society, to believe that the social order in which it finds itself always did exist, and to bend all its energies to obtaining such ameliorations of its lot within existent society as will make that lot more bearable. At this stage of society the subject class, as far as its own aspirations are concerned, may be reckoned as a conservative force.

In the third period the subject class becomes revolutionary, recks little of the past for inspiration, but, building itself upon the achievements of the present, confidently addresses itself to the conquest of the future. It does so because the development of the framework of society has revealed to it its relative importance, revealed to it the fact that within its grasp has grown, unconsciously to itself, a power which, if intelligently applied, is sufficient to overcome and master society at large.

As a classic illustration of this conception of the history of the mental development of the revolt against social oppression, we might glance at the many peasant revolts recorded in European history. As we are now aware, common ownership of land was at one time the basis of society all over the world. Our fathers not only owned their land in common, but in many ways practiced a common ownership of the things produced. In short, tribal communism was at one time the universally existent order. In such a state of society there existed a degree of freedom that no succeeding order has been able to parallel, and that none will be able to, until the individualistic order of today gives way to the Industrial Commonwealth, the Workers' Republic, of the future. How that ancient order broke up it is no part of my task to tell. What

I do wish to draw your attention to, is that for hundreds, for a thousand years after the break up of that tribal communism, and the reduction to serfdom of the descendants of the formerly free tribesmen, all the efforts of the revolting serfs were directed to a destruction of the new order of things and to a rehabilitation of the old. Take as an example the various peasant wars of Germany, the Jacquerie of France, or the revolt of Wat Tyler and John Ball in England as being the best known; examine their rude literature in such fragments as have been preserved, study their speeches as they have been recorded even by their enemies, read the translations of their songs, and in all of them you will find a passionate harking back to the past, a morbid idealizing of the status of their fathers, and a continued exhortation to the suffering people to destroy the present in order that, in some vague and undefined manner, they might reconstitute the old.

The defeat of the peasantry left the stage clear for the emergence of the bourgeoisie as the most important subject class and for the development of that second period of which I have spoken. Did it develop? Well, in every account we read of the conflicts between the nobility and the burghers in their guilds and cities we find that the aggressive part was always taken by the former and that wherever a revolt took place, the revolting guild merchants and artisans justified their act by an appeal to the past privileges which had been abrogated and the restoration of which formed the basis of their claims, and their only desire if

54

successful in revolt. One of the most curious illustrations of this mental condition is to be found in the 'History of the Rise of the Dutch Republic' by Motley [1], in which that painstaking historian tells how the Netherlands in their revolt against the Spanish Emperor continued for a generation to base their claims upon the political status of the provinces under a former Emperor, made war upon the Empire with troops levied in the name of the Emperor, and led by officers whose commissions were made out by the rebel provinces in the name of the Sovereign they were fighting against. This mental condition lasted in England until the great Civil War, which ended by leaving Charles I without a head, and the bourgeoisie, incarnated in Cromwell, firmly fixed in the saddle; in France it lasted till the Revolution. In both countries it was abandoned, not because of any a priori reasoning upon its absurdity nor because some great thinker had evolved a better scheme - but because the growth of the industrial system had made the capitalist class realize that they could at any moment stop the flow of its life-blood, so to speak, and from so realizing it was but a short mental evolution to frame a theory of political action which proclaimed that the capitalist class was the nation, and all its enemies the enemies of the nation at large. The last period of that social evolution had been reached, the last mental stage of the transition from feudal ownership to capitalist property.

Now let me apply this reading of history to the development of the working class under capitalism and find out what lessons it teaches us, of value in our present struggle. Passing by the growth of the working class under nascent capitalism, as it belongs more to the period I have just dealt with than to the present subject, and taking up working class history from the point marked by the introduction of machinery to supplant hand labor - a perfectly correct standpoint for all practical purposes - we find in the then attitude of the workers an exemplification of the historical fidelity of our conception. Suffering from the miseries attendant upon machine labor, the displacement of those supplanted and the scandalous overworking of those retained, the workers rioted and rebelled in a mad effort to abolish machinery and restore the era of hand labor. In a word, they strove to revert to past conditions, and their most popular orators and leaders were they who pictured in most glowing terms the conditions prevalent in the days of their fathers.

They were thus on the same mental plane as those medieval peasants who, in their revolt, were fired by the hope of restoring the primitive commune. And just as in the previously cited case, the inevitable failure of this attempt to reconstruct the past was followed in another generation by movements which accepted the social order of their day as permanent, and looked upon their social status as wage-slaves as fixed and immutable in the eternal order of things. To this category belongs the trade union movement in all its history. As the struggles of the serfs and burghers in the middle ages were directed to no higher aim than the establishing of better relations between these struggling classes and their feudal overlords, as during those ages the division of society into ruling classes of king, lords, and church resting upon a basis of the serfdom of the producers, was accepted by all in spite of the perpetual recurrences of civil wars between the various classes, so, in capitalist society, the trade unionists, despite strikes, lock-outs, and black lists, accepted the employing class as part and parcel of a system which was to last through all eternity.

The rise of Industrial Unionism is the first sign that that - the second stage of the mental evolution of our class - is rapidly passing away. And the fact that it had its inception amongst men actually engaged in the work of trade union organization, and found its inspiration in a recognition of the necessities born of the struggles of the workers, and not in the theories of any political party - this fact is the most cheering sign of the legitimacy of its birth and the most hopeful augury of its future. For we must not forget that it is not the theorists who make history; it is history in its evolution that makes the theorists. And the roots of history are to be found in the workshops, fields, and factories. It has been remarked that Belgium was the cockpit of Europe because within its boundaries have been fought out many of the battles between the old dynasties; in like manner we can say that the workshop is the cockpit of civilization because in the workshop has been and will be fought out those battles between the new and the old methods of production, the issues of which change the face and the history of the world.

I have said that the capitalist class became a revolutionary class when it realized that it held control of the economic heart of the nation. I may add when the working class is in the same position, it will also as a class become revolutionary, it will also give effective political expression to its economic strength. The capitalist class grew into a political party when it looked around and found itself in control of the things needed for the life of the individual and the State, when it saw that the ships carrying the commerce of the nation were its own, when it saw that the internal traffic of the nation was in the hands of its agents, when it saw that the feeding, clothing and sheltering of the ruling class depended upon the activities of the subject class, when it saw itself applied to to furnish finance to equip the armies and fleets of the kings and nobles, in short, when the capitalist class found that all the arteries of commerce, all the agencies of production, all the mainsprings of life in fact, passed through their hands as blood flows through the human heart - then and only then did capital raise the banner of political revolt and from a class battling for concessions became a class leading its forces to the mastery of society at large.

This leads me to the last axiom of which I wish you to grasp the significance. It is this, that the fight for the conquest of the political state is not the battle, it is only the echo of the battle. The real battle is the battle being fought out every day for the power to control industry and the gauge of the progress of that battle is not to be found in the number of voters making a cross beneath the symbol of a political party, but in the number of these workers who enrol themselves in an industrial organization with the definite purpose of making themselves masters of the industrial equipment of society in general.

That battle will have its political echo, that industrial organization will have its political expression. If we accept the definition of working class political action as that which brings the workers as a class into direct conflict with the possessing class AS A CLASS, and keeps them there, then we must realize that NOTHING CAN DO THAT SO READILY AS ACTION AT THE BALLOT BOX. Such action strips the working class movement of all traces of such sectionalism as may, and indeed must, cling to strikes and lock-outs, and emphasizes the class character of the Labor Movement. IT IS THEREFORE ABSOLUTELY INDISPENSABLE FOR THE EFFICIENT TRAINING OF THE WORKING CLASS ALONG CORRECT LINES THAT ACTION AT THE BALLOT BOX SHOULD ACCOMPANY ACTION IN THE WORKSHOP.

I am convinced that this will be the ultimate formation of the fighting hosts of Labor. The workers will be industrially organized on the economic field and until that organization is perfected, whilst the resultant feeling of class-consciousness is permeating the minds of the workers, the Socialist Party will carry on an independent campaign of education and attack upon the political field, and as a consequence will remain the sole representative of the Socialist idea in politics. But as industrial organization grows, feels its strength, and develops the revolutionary instincts of its members there will grow also the desire for a closer union and identification of the two wings of the army of Labor. Any attempt prematurely to force this identification would only defeat its own purpose, and be fraught with danger alike to the economic and the political wing. Yet it is certain that such attempts will be of continual recurrence and multiply in proportion to the dissatisfaction felt at the waste of energy involved in the division of forces. Statesmanship of the highest kind will be required to see that this union shall take place only under the proper conditions and at the proper moment for effective action. Two things must be kept in mind, viz., that a Socialist Political Party not emanating from the ranks of organized Labor is, as Karl Marx phrased it, simply a Socialist sect, ineffective for the final revolutionary act, but that also the attempt of craft organized unions to create political unity before they have laid the foundation of industrial unity in their own, the economic field, would be an instance of putting the cart before the horse. But when that foundation of industrial union is finally secured then nothing can prevent the union of the economic and political forces of Labor. I look forward to the time when every economic organization will have its Political Committee, just as it has its Organization Committee or its Strike Committee, and when it will be counted to be as great a crime, as much an act of scabbery to act against the former as against any of the latter. When that time comes we will be able to count our effective vote before troubling the official ballot-box, simply by counting our membership in the allied organizations; we will be able to estimate our capacity for the revolutionary act of Social Transformation simply by taking stock of the number of industries we control and their importance relative to the whole social system, and when we find that we control the strategic industries in society, then society must bend to our will - or break. In our organizations we will have Woman Suffrage, whether governments like it or not, we will also have in our own organizations a pure and uncorrupted ballot, and if the official ballot of capitalist society does not purify itself of its own accord, its corruption can only serve to blind the eyes of our enemies, and not to hide our strength from ourselves.

Compare the political action of such a body with that of any party we know. Political parties are composed of men and women who meet together to formulate a policy and programme to vote upon. They set up a political ticket in the hope of getting people, most of whom they do not know, to vote for them, and when that vote is at last cast, it is cast by men whom they have not organized, do not know, and cannot rely upon to use in their own defense. We have proven that such a body can make propaganda, and good propaganda, for socialist principles, but it can never function as the weapon of an industrially organized working class. To it, such a party will always be an outside body, a body not under its direct control, but the political weapon of the Industrially Organized Working Class will be a weapon of its own forging and wielded by its own hand. I believe it to be incumbent upon organized Labor to meet the capitalist class upon every field where it can operate to our disadvantage. Therefore I favor direct attacks upon the control of governmental powers through the ballot-box, but I wish to see these attacks supported by the economic Organization. In short, I believe that there is no function performed by a separate political party that the economic organization cannot help it perform much better and with greater safety to working class interests. Let us be clear as to the function of Industrial Unionism. That function is to build up an industrial republic inside the shell of the political State, in order that when that industrial republic is fully organized it may crack the shell of the political State and step into its place in the scheme of the universe. But in the process of upbuilding, during the period of maturing, the mechanism of the political State can be utilized to assist in the formation of the embryo Industrial Republic. Or, to change the analogy, we might liken the position of the Industrial Republic in its formative period towards political society, to the position of the younger generation towards the generation passing away. The younger accepts the achievements of the old, but gradually acquires strength to usurp its functions until the new generation is able to abandon the paternal household and erect its own. While doing so, it utilizes to the fullest all the privileges of its position. So the Industrial Unionist will function in a double capacity in capitalist society. In his position as a citizen in a given geographical area, he will use his political voting power in attacks upon the political system of capitalism, and in his position as a member of the Industrial Union he will help in creating the economic power which in the fullness of time will overthrow that political system, and replace it by the Industrial Republic.

My contentions along these lines do not imply by any means that I regard immediate action at the ballot box by the economic organization as essential, although I may regard it as advisable. As I have already indicated, the proletarian revolution will in that respect most likely follow the lines of the capitalist revolutions in the past.

In Cromwellian England, in Colonial America, in Revolutionary France the real political battle did not begin until after the bourgeoisie, the capitalist class, had become the dominant class in the nation. Then they sought to conquer political power in order to allow their economic power to function freely. It was no mere coincidence but a circumstance born of the very nature of things, woven, so to speak, in the warp and woof of fate, that in all the three countries the signal for the revolution was given by the ruling class touching the bourgeoisie in the one part that was calculated to arouse them as a class, and at the same time demonstrate their strength. That one sensitive part was their finance, their ownership of the sinews of war. In England it was over the question of taxes, of ship money, that Hampden first raised the standard of revolt whose last blow was struck at Whitehall when the king's head rolled in the gutter. In America it was over the question of taxes, and again the capitalist class were united, until a new nation was born to give them power. In France it was the failure of the king to raise taxes that led to the convocation of the States General, which assembly first revealed to the French capitalists their power as a class and set their feet upon the revolutionary path. In all three countries the political rebellion was but the expression of the will of a class already in possession of economic power. This is in conformity with the law of human evolution, that the new system can never overthrow the old, until it itself is fully matured and able to assume all the useful functions of the thing it is to dethrone.

In the light of such facts, and judging by such reasoning, we need not exercise our souls over the question of the date of the appearance of the Industrial Organizations of Labor upon the electoral field. Whether we believe, as I believe, that the electoral field offers it opportunities it would be criminal to ignore, or believe, as some do, that electoral action on the part of the economic organizations is at present premature, one thing we can be agreed upon, if we accept the outline of history I have just sketched, viz., that it is necessary to remember that at the present stage of development all actions of our class at the ballot box are in the nature of mere preliminary skirmishes, or educational campaigns and that the conquest of political power by the working class waits upon the conquest of economic power, and must function through the economic organization.

Hence, reader, if you belong to the working class your duty is clear. Your union must be perfected until it embraces every one who toils in the service of your employer, or as a unit in your industry. The fact that your employers find it necessary to secure the services of any individual worker is or ought to be that individual's highest and best title to be a member of your union. If the boss needs him you need him more. You need the open union and the closed shop if you ever intend to control the means and conditions of life. And, as the champion of your class upon the political field, as the ever active propagandist of the idea of the Working Class, as the representative and embodiment of the social principle of the future, you need the Socialist Party. The Future of Labor is bound up with the harmonious development of those twin expressions of the forces of progress; the Freedom of Labor will be born of their happily consummated union.

Further reading – Socialist Classics

Unit 1 – Short introductory works

1. The Communist Manifesto (1848) Karl Marx and Friedrich Engels

2. Wage Labour and Capital (1847) Karl Marx

3. Value, Price and Profit (1865) Karl Marx

4. Socialism: Utopian and Scientific (1880) Friedrich Engels

5. The German Ideology (1846) Karl Marx and Friedrich Engels

6. Anarchism and Socialism (1895) Georgi Plekhanov

7. No Compromise, No Political Trading (1899) Wilhelm Liebknecht

8. Reform or Revolution (1900) Rosa Luxemburg

9. Leninism or Marxism? (1904) Rosa Luxemburg

10. Socialism Made Easy (1909) James Connolly